Praise for
City on the Second Floor

Matt Sedillo brings poetic fire to the burn through the issues – avarice, mediocrity, lies, gentrification, labor, loneliness, class conflict and others – most officially-sanctioned "poets" ignore in the name of the ice cold fakery that calls itself "poetry" in the United States. Thankfully, Sedillo burns down the house built out of the illusion of democracy, of the "literary". In this sense, he brings necessary fire.

> — **Roberto Lovato**, Author of *Unforgetting, A Memoir of Family, Migration, Gangs and Revolution in the Americas*

Sedillo is the Carlos the Jackal of poetry.

> — **Geo Maher**, Author of *A World Without Police*

Matt Sedillo is a poet during times of unveiling, when the source of what makes this country and world tick--and fall part--becomes revealed to millions.

> — **Luis Javier Rodriguez**, Author of *Always Running: La Vida Loca: Gang Days in L.A.* and *It Calls You Back: An Odyssey Through Love, Addiction, Revolutions, and Healing*

I studied with Ginsberg, I drank with Bukowski, and now I've met the new master. Run and hide, white boy, Sedillo writes with a switchblade. the best political poet alive – and everything is political.

> — **Greg Palast**, Author of *How Trump Stole 2020: The Hunt for America's Vanished Voters*

CITY ON THE
SECOND FLOOR

FLOWERSONG
PRESS

poems by
Matt Sedillo

FlowerSong Press
Copyright © 2022 by Matt Sedillo
ISBN: 978-1-953447-89-0
Library of Congress Control Number: 2021953540

Published by FlowerSong Press
in the United States of America.
www.flowersongpress.com

Cover Art by Giovanni Solis
Cover Art Design by Edward Vidaurre
Set in Adobe Garamond Pro

NOTICE: SCHOOLS AND BUSINESSES
FlowerSong Press offers copies of this book at quantity discount with bulk
purchase for educational, business, or sales promotional use. For information,
please email the Publisher at info@flowersongpress.com.

To my father, who taught me to play chess… and then never let me win.

FOREWORD

Among the various tropes in history and in biographies is the tale of the renegade who forsakes convention – or is forsaken by it. There in solitude the renegade contemplates, meditates, sulks, cries, broods, and studies. Torturous and impositional as this is, he is blessed to only be scarred by the experience and gain vision and understanding of himself, of others, of others in himself and himself in others. A walk-about, a vision-quest, a pilgrimage, a fast, a dharma-bum, imprisonment, on-the-run, a motorcycle diary, double-consciousness, migration, nepantla, a rabbit's hole, or whatever brand of exile and Augustinian flirtation with the divide between life and death, the poet – in this case – is stronger for having survived and emerged with a Quin-ian creed convinced of his distinction and convinced that he sees deep into the way of things.

I stretch language a bit – and maybe just a bit – to say that Matt Sedillo's understandings are drawn from hell. He knows its streets, its traffic, its walls, language, graffiti, its buildings, its libraries, its birds... each dusted in asbestos, smeared in grease, yellowed bymonoxide. There in this pit he has traversed the fine line between cynicism and suspicion, ignorance and knowledge. And from there our erudite "poet laureate of the struggle" has returned with an understanding that is no commodity for some future exchange on some promise about whose vacuity he is, anyway, well aware. Drawn as his understanding is from his descent it is here illustrated in Galean-esque manner and shared in impatient and righteous cadence – sometimes gently and individually, sometimes loudly and collectively. Odd that whatever it is he might say seems hyperbolic. Odd because it isn't. It is, as is often said on Chicano streets, la mera neta. Imagine that.

Each one of the poems of this new collection of poetry (and one play) is incisive, each one more than telling. Educators that work in schools where Chicana/o students are the disproportionate demographic – which is often the case in whatever school they happen to be a demographic – ought to be especially piqued by his Serling-esque ode to so-called Hispanic Serving Institutions, what segregated colleges and universities are conventionally called. Where he draws from critique of post-war fetishizations and the destructive practices of consumption, he challenges us in the pages that reader has at hand to called. Where he draws from critique of post-war fetishizations and the destructive practices of consumption, he challenges us in the pages that reader has at hand to see how hold-over schools from the post-war era and so-called Hispanic students positioned in them are en route to obsoletion if consumption – i.e., "purchasing-power" – is what ultimately impels their schooling. This game of learning where lives are gambled and whose cards are assimilation, integration, purchasing power, and debt is born in backrooms and gambling halls where bankers, politicians, and university administrators hedge that a bill-of-goods, tenuous as their ideas of ethnicity and empire are, justify the risk. Sedillo's dystopian poem of Chicana/o higher education reminds us that if there is no stable and steady job then the better industrial bet is to tear down schools and build more prisons. A heady reminder that those served in these so-called institutions may really not be its students. Already more is nationally spent on imprisonment than in schooling and California, the state with the greatest concentration of so-called Hispanics, spends most on imprisonment than any other state in the nation – la mera neta!

If this book's title was mine to make I would have drawn from the lines of one of its poems – "…a storm is brewing/And you have/Been warned." After all, its poetry and one play are about the ways that the experiences of working people and sometimes-working people are mistakenly felt as one working man's or sometimes-working man's blues. Ready yourself, then, for a "Lords Prayer" turned on its head. One that has brushed Christian mysticism and superstition aside to bare the city, this hell, these Bobcat Fires and its demon lords here on earth. Along the way you will become an element in Sedillo's sometimes didactic poetry though always necessary given our contemporary culture of fast food, fast words, short orders and short thoughts. None, of these things is really substantive. Each is damaging if palliative, hollow, and empty of sustenance. And many of us as its consumers and producers are all the while sedate, tranquil, meditating – in yogic pose even – as the future thins. Sedillo's poetry is a necessary kick in the ass – "Wake up!" it seems to say.

— **Dr. Jose Prado**, Professor of Sociology
at Cal State Dominguez Hills

CONTENTS

Bonus materials

CITY ON THE SECOND FLOOR

Post

You know it seems like just yesterday
Municipalities raised cities
Built nuclear families
Associations of sturdy pockets
        A two-car garage, chicken in every pot
    A military expansion
           A man on the moon and a finger on the button
   Tomorrow doesn't show up all at once
        But when it does
Liquidate the pension
Automate the factory
Auction off the options
Don't worry bout me
    I worry free
Free-lance contingency
Smiling at your service to gig economy
     Side hustle, millennial, post industrial standard
Hire me as an adjunct
Fire me as contingent
Into a city I cannot afford to live in
Tell me my credit score
Better yet, tell me yours
Promise me the world, then show me the door
        I was not
        Born
        Angry
I was abandoned
I am your velveteen rabbit
The drying paint of Saturn eating his children
Neoliberalism feasting on the marrow
Of the past and the present, the jobs of tomorrow, gone today
Born sometime after the foreclosure
   Tell me another for the fire
          Tell me the one
       Where I killed the economy

L.A. is Full of Pigs

Los Angeles is falling apart
In the streets, in the suburbs
                                        In the wind
                    In a barely kept Hollywood bathroom
Wheezing, vomiting, coughing up blood
The past few days, these past few years
                    I have spread myself across this sprawl
                                        And now fear this drive may kill me
May kill us all and I wander
                    Over to general hospital
        Between whose walls desperation wears in high concentration
upon the faces of the shopworn
And prematurely ill alike as they await upon news of illness they cannot afford to have
                    Survival without insurance
                    This may take a while
            Los Angeles
                    Is full of untold misery
A homeless man sleeps next to me and I can smell the years of hard distance
between who he is now
                    And who he may have been
        And all that stands between him and the bitter wind
Is chance, is the kindness of a night nurse who will let him sleep in peace
                    Los Angeles is full of good people
                    Who from time to time
                    Can turn a blind eye
                    To killer policy
And I wonder how many more bounced checks, free clinics, carry cash
                                        And leave the account in the negative
                    Stand between me and him, me and the bitter wind and if so
            Where would I go from Venice to San Francisco
        There is an outright war on the homeless
        A war on the dispossessed, there are fewer and fewer options
They got shelters for women and children, all inadequate
But for me just man up homeboy
To that concrete pillow
To that cardboard blanket
And freeze your ass to death

4

Yes, this city will leave you to die
      On the same stretch of sidewalk where banks stretch into the sky
And I wonder as even now skid row Is being gentrified
          As this city
          As this system
          As the pigs
          Push people
          Past poverty
          Past hunger
        Past homelessness
      Towards the very edge of existence
          On Skid Row
              Where all the so-called complexities of an economy
    Are laid bare, where the rich are literally stacked upon the poor
        Los Angeles
      Is full of grotesque absurdity
Especially on skid row
Where they spend millions
Annually policing the misery of people with nowhere to go
Because when your pockets are empty
      And you aint got nothing
        And change is just not coming
        There is no real difference
Between a booming metropolis and a barren desert
And the world of money
Passes by you
Passes through you
    As though you
Were just part
    Of the scenery
Protected in the knowledge
They are serviced by pigs
Who speak the language of violence
The language
Of the nightstick
The language
Of untold misery
That will beat you for begging
      Beat you for sleeping
      Beat you for breathing
Beat you
For doing whatever it is you need to do

To survive the night
In the bitter wind
Los Angeles
Is full of pigs

6

Vanderbilt

Company town from the ground up
     Vanderbilt
With the command of the will of millions at hand
        Not tycoons, titans nor captains
           No
       Gods amongst men
  On your knees
   Make your way
       Your bones
          Your peace
 Pay your dues
  Your taxes
    Their fees
       Receive, whatever small consultation you can in the time that you have
        Pay the piper your saving grace then leave instruction for your grave
Cause on the fifth day
       Carnegie rebuilds in his image
  Four walls make a factory
      Three meals, a union contract
Rockefeller will have you shot where you stand
       There are only two ways this can end
This is life or death, loaded
             One nation under the gun
  There will be blood
Their will be done
  Their will of rail, steel, oil
   Drill the soil
  Poison the ocean
  Puncture the sky
From the commanding heights

           Harbingers
         Of greed and death
      The makers of the modern world
        Watching it burn
        Gods amongst men

Pope of Broadway

An Arab, an Italian, a Jew, a Puerto Rican, an Inuit an American Indian, a Mongolian
And a Mexican

Walk into a bar

Anthony Quinn orders a drink
The man the myth the mural the Greek
Citizen of the world, the Pope of Broadway, patron saint of acting while ethnically ambiguous
For ambiguity and ethnicity both reside in the eye of producer
Cliff Curtis, Oscar Isaac, give me two first names and I'll give you the swarthy world
For every leading man is a hero and to every hero a journey
And to every journey, a tropical sidekick
Damp sand to light brick give me a bowler and a turtleneck or tanning bed and bronzer
And I'll give you a brown man for every clime and season
Spelled

M
a
n
Melanin as needed

And I know this town, know it better than it knows me, grew in its shadow
Sun Valley day trips to Melrose and Sunset
Hollywood nights on Highland
My brother, our friends, two cousins
Brown kids from the valley walking the stars in a tinsel town
Down an avenue
of dreams, waiting on Columbus
My brother had us convince,
Whatever it was
We had it
First to find work
Cholo number nine
Loco number three
Vato number six
We raised a toast to a sky with no limits
Team captain said my boys you are all up next
First and only speaking gig
Immortalized as an Armenian mechanic
Vato hasn't found work since

And I know this country
I know it better than it knows itself
What it likes
What it hides
What it ignores
What it won't admit
And what that says
Heard a story that
When Anthony Quinn married in to the DeMille family
It was on the condition that his very Mexican family would not be attending
the wedding
And that's the ticket, the price of admission, what they are buying and you had best be selling
And let me tell you one thing
When Dallas, Minneapolis, Ann Arbor, Orlando, Toledo, Scranton Ohio sends their people
They don't send their best
They're vain
They're shallow
They're narcissists
And some of them I imagine are good waiters
Flight of the sociopaths
Transplants turned cynics chasing down plans, hopes and ambitions
On roads paved in ways I would never even begin to dream to imagine
Talking only to themselves, defining a place by all they claim it is not but it's them
Fake, fakes, fake as fuck, fuck them
They don't know this town, this region the history
Hell they don't even know the valley
The valley is swap meets, car shows, the 118, San Fernando Road
Ghost stories on Gravity Hill, the 5, Pedro de Pacas
The legend of Richie Valens, the mural of Danny Trejo and that's as real as it gets
The valley is me, mi tios, my cousins, a laptop connected to the television watching
Andy Ruiz defeat Anthony Joshua for the heavyweight championship of the world
Our world is Andy the Destroyer being mocked for his appearance
And Ruiz said every Mexican has a dream
Underestimated
Overlooked
Mocked
Exploited
Neglected
Disrespected
Yet here we stand
With more talent than you ever began to dream to imagine
For every Mexican is a hero

And to every hero a journey
And to every journey a purpose
And to every purpose a sense dignity
And may every ounce dignity
Be poured into a dream
Never forgetting the compromises and sacrifices
How this road was paved
Emerging from the shadows on the shoulders of giants
On some brighter day
With the Pope of Broadway
Dancing
In celebration of it all

City on the Second Floor

There is a city on the second floor
An international destination
Whose entrance is prohibited
To all those appearing
Too poor for travel
Where commerce crosses
Bridges of wire and concrete
Just above the street light
Rises an economy of scale
Where buildings and offices
Connect to disconnect from the world below
Here
In the space between
Worker and destination
Conversation spins profit
And no one moves without reason
And no one speaks without purpose
Here
The word is stillborn
A commodity
And the world dies anew
While working stiff spend wages
In cheap imitation
Of their exploitation
Arrogant
Delusional
Walking dead
Laughingly dreaming
Of a penthouse suite
They will never reach
While staring down from terraces
Towards the street below

The Rich

The rich, well they're not like you and me
They see an opportunity and they grab it reach for the stars
And they, put 'em in their pocket
Company stays in the red
But they're backed by the government
Snort the public dime into lines of pure profit
Research and development

The rich, well they're a different breed
Champagne wishes and caviar dreams
Thoroughbred stallions, quarter billion mansions on the sea
Deepwater Horizon
Blood diamonds
Golden parachutes
Silicon messiahs
Feasting on endangered species
Served on silver platters in winter palaces carved from the tips of icebergs
Six-figure charters
Vulture capital
Million-dollar cufflinks plucking life like an apple
Insured by suicide nets
Lifestyles of the criminally negligent
But you haven't lived
Until you've launched a car into space for no fucking reason
Now that's what I call freedom

The rich, well here's how it is
Dollars and cents
Trademark and rent
Facts and figures
Lines on a ledger
Derivatives and debt
Building the future
Increasing productivity
Union busting back
To the hundred-hour work week
Trimming the fat

Producing monopolies
With real money shortages and bets
And that my friend is how the rich stay rich
While the rest, make poor decisions
And it's pure ecstasy
Living in the lap of luxury
Pushing pharmaceuticals
At the markup
The market
Will bear your body
To its altar
At a life-or-death bargain
The gospel
Of wealth
Cause it is what it is
And that's all it's ever been

The less we spend
The more we keep

You see the rich
And the poor
Well, they're just like you and me

Two hands
Two feet
The sky
The sea
And everything between
One heart that beats
And the time
To make the most of it
So, you'll find no sympathy
Reaching into these deep pockets
All we ever asked was our fair share
And God damn it, that's all of it
So, while you're out in the streets screaming for peace and justice
We're sleeping in satin sheets dreaming free and guiltless over oceans and tariffs
liquidating pensions then off to bid on porcelain and portraits at billion dollar auctions
You know you need us
You know we're selling your secrets
You know you still send us DNA kits
Watching the puppets
On television

Debate freedom free speech
　　　　Fascism, democracy while we reach into the earth
And fuel the economy
　　　With space stations
　　　　　　Yes, space stations
　　　　　　　　　Hydrating the red planet
We're gonna survive this lava pit
So you got pots and pans
We got deeds and plans
　　　　　　　Chopping down rainforest
　　　　　　　　　　　　Colonizing the moon
　　　　　We're the rich, who the fuck are you
　　　　　We'll privatize the water supply
　　　　　　Then copyright the tears
　　　　　　　Falling
　　　　　　　From
　　　　　　　Your
　　　　　　　　Eyes
　　　Burn it all down
　　What the hell you talking about
The icecaps are already melting
　　　　　　You wanna start some shit
　　　　　　　　　　　　Eat the rich
We're already killing your kids
One carbon footprint
One gas house emission
One oil rig
One naval ship
One free
Trade
Agreement at a time
　　　　　　And we'll get away with it too
　　　　　　　　　Nothing we say or
do
　　　　Is ever held against us
　　　Haven't you been paying attention
　　　　　We're rich

City Hall

And so it is carved
To the city's halls
That the letter of the law of the land stands alone
But that's just a longstanding joke
Like the rich and poor stand before the letter of the law just alike
In the citadel where robed men divine
The newest testament
To all that can
And cannot be fought
What time can be sold
And how it can be bought
Now stand at attention
Now honor your judgement
Now lock fingers behind your head
Now move to your knees and remove any and all signs of contempt
Hands behind your back
Do not resist
This is a nation of law

Storm Warnings

When it all finally goes down
When the titanic
Finally sinks
When there is nowhere
Left to hide the money
When the alps finally melt
When Switzerland
Becomes a barren desert
And the Caymans
Are buried
Miles below
Sea level
The fortune five hundred
Will set up
Tax shelters
On the moon

A storm is brewing
From the winds of Fukushima
From the ash of three-mile island
From the criminal negligence
The killing plunder
You can hear the distant thunder
Strip the earth to feed industry
Pillage the country
To please the city
Milk the city
To engorge the capital
Make weapons capable
Of destroying the planet
Turn profit
From tankers that poison
The ocean
From factories
That darken the sky
And a storm is brewing
From the ghosts of Bhopal

The graveyard of Exxon Valdez
From the soot that is rising
Out of an industrial revolution
A commercial revolution
A Chevy revolution
Inviting you to
Join the mad chorus
As the rubber hits the road
Show
Those
Who would live
In natural rhythm
Raise children
To the tune
Of a rain drop's song
The savagery the mechanical man is made of
Let them know
That a hard acid rain is going to fall
From the Niger Delta
To the Cuyahoga
From the holes
In the o zone
Over Mexico city
New Delhi
Cairo
From the geological crime scene
Of the river Ganges
To the bitter harvest
Of terminator seeds
From the mountain tops
Chopped off
In the heart
Of Appalachia
From the Canadian tar sands
To the coal seams of the badlands
To the polluted streams of Gasland
There is nowhere to run
Nowhere to hide
No shelter this time
And a storm is a brewing
And you had best beware
For what profits a man

Should he gain the world
But cannot breathe its air
And this is no way to live
Because this land
This sky
The sea
Was made
Just as you and as me
For us and for we
And for them and for they
Who are not yet born
Who have yet to hear
A single raindrop song
And our hearts are stirring
Our feet are marching
Our choir is rising
So to those who would
Turn this earth to wasteland
Our home
To landmine
To save a nickel
Or scrape thin dimes
With their eyes set
On mountains of profit
Well you had best
Batten down the hatches
Cross your fingers
And lock your doors
Because a storm is brewing
And you have
Been warned

After the Revolution

                          After the revolution
                              There will be gulags
          And shallow graves
                  After the revolution
    Known white supremacists
Shall be taken and beaten
  In the town squares and county fairs
Of the shiny new people's republic with the confiscated toothbrushes of reeducated libertarians
                  After the revolution
    Silicon Valley executives will appear on state sponsored commercial free reality television
                  Survival island of the fittest
          Where the 1 percent may enter
                              And none shall leave
          Our revolution will not be a drab gray affair
                  There will singing
                  Dancing
                  Laughing
                  Pissing
              On the graves
                  Of all who had made the world as it was in the time before

The Sky

To a beautiful Brown mobile proletariat native to the continent
Displaced by imperial capital
That lays claim to clay
Claim to soil
Claim to all that stands upon it
To all that grows out of it

Crossing rivers and canyons
Defying textbook explanation
The flight of the monarch butterfly
Represents freedom, represents movement
Guided by ancestral knowledge
Along a path set generations before them
And isn't that just like

butterflies
Imperialists
Industrialists
Men of arms
Made up of war

Lay claim to the sky

Declare no fly zones
Make cults of drones
Declare war without cost
Drop bombs

Phosphorus gas
Depleted uranium
Napalm

Last I heard
They were building a space force
While praying to
For the money and strength
To colonize the heavens

the sky

Elephant

One morning I had awoken with tusks

Drifting in and out
Of sleep
Like so much life unseen
I knew this by feel alone
The cool air on my back
Reflections of gray
Shards of glass
I tried to recall the time before
Splintered wood
The warmth of sun
Daylight in my room
My skin
My limbs

"The emails"

I recalled
"Do not forget
The emails"

A knock on the door

No doubt
The owner of the house
I was certain
Every day she berates my appearance.
Every day fresh new criticisms
How I dress
When I leave
When I return

I work

I rent
All I ask in return
Is peace
Is silence
Now the live-in lover

Who does not work

Who does not rent
Who mocks my appearance
How I move through the world

Bulldog of a man
Barks at my door
Howls in my room
Unsolicited opinion
More threats
More stress

"Work" they say

"Dress" they say

"Emails do not forget your emails"

I have broken the bed
I cannot get out of a bed
That I have broken

This isn't fair

This isn't right
It never was
I cannot see the light
A new voice joins

The choir of demands

More pounding

"Wake up to work
Your emails
Do not forget
Your emails"
"I am your landlord"
"I am your office boss"
"She is your landlord"
"He is your office boss"

Hands pound
Voices boom
Demand
Demand
I cannot move
This isn't fair
It never was
More threats
More stress
The pounding continues
Demand
Demand

"Your emails"
"Do not forget your emails"

The pounding
The pounding
The pounding
Demand
Demand
Demand
Demand
Demand
The demand of light
The door falls
The landlord gasps
The live in lover gasps
The office boss gasps
The office boss cries out

"My God there's an elephant in the room"

Gerald Ford

December twenty-sixth two thousand and six
A homeless man shuffles down the way
Of Main Street, Downtown anywhere USA
It is the same day
Gerald Ford has died…

So, I am walking down the street
And I am thinking
They finally did it
Day after Christmas
The flag is at half-mast
The politicians the preachers
The admen
They've moved on
They killed him off
Jesus Christ, well, he's dead
Which is a big fucking problem
For me anyhow
People are already broke
And I am trying
To cash in on
Whatever's left of
Their giving spirit
First tip, never beg
That's right
There's a right
And a wrong way
To do everything
Secondly and more importantly
Never let on
You have nowhere to go
Try and convince 'em
You have somewhere you call home
See anyone can end up stranded
But it takes a special case
To have absolutely nothing
No one, nowhere, no place

Like
Maybe they'll think you deserve it
So, I hit up this kid
Hey listen, look I am not
Really from around here
He flinches steps back
So, I ask
Hey man
What's up the flag?
Hallelujah!!!
I say
Jesus lives and he saves
Next year there will be soup and sweaters
Guess things aren't looking so hot
For Gerald Ford though
Day after Christmas
And people are crying
Flying the flag low
For Gerald fucking Ford
Yeah, you tell me when Chevy Chase dies
And like with either one of those clowns
This shit ain't that funny
'Cause, you see, I am dying out here
I am dying out here
But all I ever seem to hear
Is that we got problems
With the youth
Far too many of them
Trying to be hard on the street
Well see I got the exact opposite problem
These streets have been
Pretty goddamn hard on me
Because with or without a weapon drawn
I have slept in alleys and tunnels
Where the wind cuts you to shreds
Blows through you like cannonballs
Yeah, I am so down and out
It's downright criminal
Cause whether it's security guards
Punk kids or the fucking cops
All fighting back ever gets you
Is one thing

Can you guess?
More fucking cops
And all the businesses, the police unions
The politicians
Well they are all in unison
We are far and away
The city's biggest problem
Well, bring it on then you Nazis
What's your final solution?
'Cause I ain't going nowhere
Because I can't
Bet you wanna know how I got here right?
Well fuck that
'Cause, see, I got some questions
And I want some answers
And not in the sweet hereafter
Or in some final chapters
Or some pie in the sky when I die
Or when I finally do run into
Jesus H. Christ
Waiting in some godforsaken
Church charity soup line
But in the here and now
Questions like
Why must I beg?
Why must I lie?
Think this couldn't happen to you?
Think you're better than me?
What's so different about
The air that you breathe?
A national day of mourning
For Gerald fucking Ford
But what good is a nation
A society
A civilization
An economy
If it can't make room for everybody?
Oh, I brought it on myself?
I did this to me?
Go fuck yourself then
Go on
Go on with your national

Day of mourning
For Gerald fucking Ford
But just answer me this
What twenty-one gun salute
Will I receive?
Or the hundreds of thousands
The millions
Just like me?
Sleeping in the street
Begging for your scraps
Living off your trash
Who will so much as
Lower their head
Or clasp their hands
When we pass?
We pass by you
Every day
And I know
You're not to blame
But neither am I
'Cause you see it's like I said
I am not really from around here
I am just trying to go home
And I'd be gladly on my way
If you could spare some change
Every little bit helps
Oh, I appreciate this I really do
Merry Christmas
God bless you

Hammurabi

I grew up on television and so did my parents
I Love Lucy
Lied to them sweetly
America's
Favorite redhead
Desires suppressed
In separate beds
Censors rest
Assured
Everything in good taste
Everything in its proper place
Every traumatic episode
Ends with the threat of Ricky's hand
Never far from Lucy's face

Beaming in glorious black and white
Wrong and right
Plot lines shade out the gray
On John Wayne's
Shining silver
City on a hill
Of guns and butter

Where every
School child's desk
Doubles as bomb shelter
Praying to the altar of the unquestioned

So
Pledge your allegiance
Seal your documents
And lock and load
Your freedom
Because it is not free
Now fall to your knees
And praise be

To the only God
In which we trust

The Atom
The Manhattan

                                        Hiroshima
                                        Nagasaki
                                 The nuclear family
                Nuclear testing
                                                        In the nuclear age

Gave way
To nuclear waste
That's me
  See
I grew up
In the eighties
               Morning in America
                    Ronald Reagan
                         And Mr. Belvedere
        Fresh at my door
     Telling me life was
                                        More than mere survival
                    That I
             Might live the good life
                                 Yet when my time came
                                             Homer Simpson
                                               Peter Griffin
                                                  Al Bundy

               Were all lying in wait
          To convince me
        I could raise a family
           In a two story
        On the single income
                                                  Of a shoes salesman
They lied
And I cry
Not for myself
But for this oncoming generation
                    Of IPAD kids
                         On the Hulu and Netflix
                    Where you pick your poison
                         But it rots your mind
                           Just the same
                         See them at cafes
                           Sit sipping
                           Job seeking
                         Asking the net

For deeper meaning

Who am I

Where do I belong

Of what use can I be

In days such as these

Kids born of go go gadgets

Wired to networks

Connected

Directed

To the latest trends

Surf the web

In search of themselves

No different

From medieval serfs

Waiting on the bells

Of the Catholic Church

For the latest in

Holy writ

Holy script

Holy this

Since

The golden rule

Of Pharaohs and Caesars

Romulus and Remus

Akbar and Alexander

Xerxes and Hammurabi

Since the days of scribes

And the books of Kings

Since they from on high

Convinced us down below

That we

Ever

Needed

Their

Code

Of law

To tell us

We were free

Precarious Rex

There is no democracy in the way of things
　　　　　There is no democracy in the way of things
　　　　　　　　　There is no
　　Democracy
　　　　　　　　　　　In the way
　　　　Of things
And tortured are the hands moved by the engine of a clock
　　　　The world as it is
　　　　Whether you like it or not
For all the world's a cage
And we men and women merely prisoners
And one man
In his time
Can do many bids
As his time begins
In name and birth certificate
With the measure of infant
With doctor's swift hand
That first humiliating scene
In the very first public act
Welcome to the world baby
You ain't seen nothing yet
Then on
To schoolyard and lunchbox
Then off to factory feed and process
Bright face
Clean teeth
Amongst others new to the fact
That there is no
Democracy in the way of things
Then on to fighter, then lover
Soldier, company man
True believer
Full of strange and tragic oaths
To a world of jealous competition
And how in this time
He shall live

Firm now in the fact
That one day
He shall die
And how on this stage
He shall dream
And how on this stage
He shall strive
Then onto eyes wise
With familiarity
That like cancer grows
As the imagination bends with the spine
In his last years
Dead man walking
Voice trembling
Silence encroaching
Eyes fading
Failure
Coming into view
As time served
Ends
This
        Strange
            Eventful
                History
Just as it began
Ashes to ashes
Dust to dust
Oblivion to oblivion
Imprisoned
Leaving nothing behind him
But measurements
To be weighed, documented
By doctor's certificate
        But let us not begin nor end
      This journey in such morbid fashion
        Let us instead
          Join our hero midstream
            Some dashed dream
Somewhere between
        Realization and acceptance
           Somewhere in the way of things

                                        Enter stage left
Precarious Rex
                        The king of debt
                Brown bagging
                                    On a splintered park bench
                        Man of letters
                    Adjunct professor
        In the valley of a saint named for an avenging angel in search of all that
went wrong
I made my way
                To the corner of mission and the sea
 Leaving the steps of the library
    Not of the jailers
Though I am no stranger
To either longstanding
And altogether
Far too public
Institutions
Of coercion
And correction
Ha-ha
And it was there
In these hours
Of early sun
                                            On route to a familiar post
                    In a favored park
        Along my morning constitutional
                            Killing time, reviving dreams
            Waiting upon
                    Some happier hour hailing from some brighter horizon
        A round or two of catching up
                        With an old colleague
Where and when
            Occurred is the wrong word
                            In this I mean to be precise
        Lest you get the wrong impression
                            Like so much in life it was a thought
returned
                                More on the contemplation on
these phantom neurons later
            Let us instead take a moment to ponder
                                            How often

33

                                    And with what mystery
Do thoughts reoccur
                How, when and at
                            What frequency
Do they begin to shape the mind
                    This no feat of rhetoric
                        No subterfuge of diction
                            No idle exercise
            No mental self-pleasure
                        These are questions
With answers
        And in them
            The composite and contours of a life
So listen now and heed this advice
                    Be guarded with that that which enters your eyes
For the stage doth inform the play
                                        Falling asleep in public
                    Is an art not a science
                    I woke up three rows removed
                From the next living soul
                                    Checked my pockets

        Losing tickets secure
            My father
        Would slap my face
    Were to see how his money
        Exchanged palms
        With such gentle ease
            Into the revelry
                Of a
                        Tuesday afternoon
            More on him later
                    For now
                Let us instead consider
The strange eventful
            History of one
                        Elias Lucky Baldwin
                            Born in the final year of
    Jacksonian Democracy with all its promise of land theft
And libertine debauchery
            When asked for a defining legacy
Baldwin Pointed to the Santa Anita Race Tracks
                And said

This was it
And that was Lucky
Early westward visionary and pioneer
Of land speculation
And underpaying Mexicans
A tradition to which my labor
Is accustomed
And a practice to which my employers
Both prior and current
Have proven themselves
Not only to be among the grandest of enthusiasts
But also, the most ardent of practitioners
Bring on the night
The after-work bar rush
That rat race towards dusk
Because the thought
That plagued my mind
The phantom neuron that could use some company
Or just some drinking
Was this
There is far too much death in this valley
Far too many odes
To the odious
The murderous
Pious
Pirates of land
Shaping the architecture
That hangs over the intersection of Route 66
And the mission system
Where you see fit
To judge this descendent of California law
Well judge as you must
Me
I prefer to run
For all the world is a tavern
And on an evening such as this
On a dare
A cantina
And we men and women merely its patrons
We have our entrances
Our exits
Sometimes a little sooner than expected

A toast
To our mothers
Our fathers
The lovers
The haters
The cynics
The decisions that made us
To those who would seek
To understand or dismiss us
Our resistance
To their instructions
To our teachers
Our doubters
Our enlisters
Our true believers
Their institutions
That would ensnare us
In prisons of velvet
To our most vicious detractors
Who would say just about any cruel thing about us
To the saboteurs and supporters
The inquisition and ignorers
To these strange
Eventful combinations
Real and imagined
Lift your glass
To the degrees on the wall
To the check in the mail
May we live
To outrun them both

But let us leave something to savor
Something to be said for the evening
Let us not prematurely dip
Into that pit of profundity
Our strange and tragic greatest hits
A review
Of all this life and surroundings
To which you and I have both born witness
Let us pick up where we have left it
Let us speak of the world
Its state of affairs
Their driving forces

Prevailing interests
Cause and effect
        Let the conversation renew
The news of the day concerning
    Some colleague
            A contemporary
That some might argue and I might rightly concur
Has been the recipient as of late of far too kind
  Far too public
                And may I add quite unmerited praise and success
        And of course
    Let us discuss
                    Just how precious little
Democracy there is in the way of things
And I tell you all this
All this and more
Life could afford
But instead
    To the greater dissatisfaction
Of patrons, prisoners
                    Participants and audience alike
            The specter of commerce
Insisted upon the conversation
Just imagine
                    An invitation to reunion with a dear friend
Only to be met with attempts to be roped in
        Into some type of
    Academic pyramid scheme
                A tenure track position
                    In Carbondale Illinois
                I would rather die
                A thousand deaths
                In all the chain restaurants
                    Of Monrovia
                    Then.....
                            I woke up in the back of a
ride share
        Better there than the jailers I suppose, though I could not help but
                            Wonder if I had left the bar of my volition
Checked my pockets
Losing tickets
Still in place

37

I am after all
A fool of
Odd and tragic
Sentiments
Checked my phone
For the time
And my destination
Seven thirty pm
Childhood home
      This fellow traveler appears in no mood
                For engagement
So I close my eyes, perchance to dream
        When half asleep
           My aspirations seem within reach
Life should not be this hard
      And now just the driver and I
        As we strike conversation
          He tells me he has three children
            He tells me hails from Michoacán
  I lie
    I say so do my parents
        He asks if I have ever been
   I have
    So in this instance
     I speak the truth
      I tell him I am a professor
         And there is light in his eyes
      And now this becomes a matter of public service
     I quickly comprise a compromise between the lies
   He needs to hear
And the ones I need to tell
       I tell him I am a very famous author
        I tell him my father is very, very proud of me
    I tell him my life is the fruit of my parent's sacrifice
I tell him
      Any time I think of them
It brings a tear to my eye
       I tell him
         His children can be anything
          To which they set their
mind
We reach Baldwin Park

We reach the home
            Where my father no longer hides his contempt
        Where my father watches television
As my mother prepares a plate
                    She asks about an American friend by which she means
White
                                        I tell her about a full-time position
in Southern Illinois
That I am very, very, very seriously considering taking
                    My mother nearly begins to cry
                    My mother runs to the other room to tell my father
the good news
                I can hear as he says
            He will believe it when sees it
            My eyes are heavy
            They scan the familiar setting
                The strange eventful beginning of me
                Portraits of the family
                Framed oil paintings
                    The legends of the home country
                    The pride of Cuauhtémoc
                    The folly of Juan Diego
                    My master's degree
                        It's place
            Somewhere in this home
Somewhere in between
                There is no democracy in the way of things

Camelot

This is a Molotov

                                        Tossed towards Camelot

This is paradise won
The rise of the sixth sun
This is myth
That is legend
A sense of direction
When you can't trust your senses
Materially historic and dialectic
Mysterious until it isn't
It is written
For the now past present
And future generations

                                                        Count seven
                                        This is that this and that shit
                                                That don't knock it
                                                Till you try it
                                                Today's hypothesis
                                                Tomorrow's science

That which remains the same
In this state of constant change
In a fit of rage
In a jilted state
In a gilded age
The spark that lights the flame
In these decades made days
                                At the risk of sounding ridiculous
                                        It's that postindustrial proletariat
Spitting back the fruit of knowledge
                                        Eat the rich
History will absolve us
                                The city was built against us
Always was
                        Even now as the city shoots up
                                The law crashes down
From the hanging courts

                                                The peerless jury

The sitting judge

The city is out for blood

Look right look left

Bands of armed men

Pledge to fraternal orders

To one another

Answer only to the call of death

In fire and memory, the city's walls rebel

Tell tales from a time

When the people arose

Though long ago

And somewhere else

Pride

Is the compromise of public life

Struck by

Those who serve

And the killers of time

The devourers of light

Parasites

This city rides by night

Runs off the sweat of the backs who work it

Laying the very brick

That walls them off

Then off to stuff the pockets

Of those who work them

The city is a field

Labor is the crop

As one building crumbles

Another scrapes the sky

Planners call it beautification and blight

Ink bleeds a cartography of hypocrisy and lies

As every next day's headline reads

A poor mother's nightmare

And a rich man's dream

The tale of all too many cities

And isn't a shame

And there was no other way

And after careful consideration

And internal investigation

The city finds no fault within itself

Tragic

Regrettable

Inevitable
                        But justifiable
    Just another day
           Another page
      Another slain
                Another shot in the back
       At the hands
       Of death squads
The city is awash with tears
 To the tale
  To die on your feet
 By parable
 By any means
  To the trajectory
   Of a Molotov tossed towards the break of dawn
               Tonight
          By prayer and proverb
           Camelot burns
                      Into the fire
                   The city bursts
                    Over the ash
       Chants and commands converge
         Through the smoke
        The hours of the prole emerge
          Wood aluminum led
           As the night set
          Would contest
The barricades
For cityscape
Of the gavel and baton's relinquished claim
                       The armory fell
                The coin crashed
         A brick
                   Shattered the chapel of print
       Cracked the mint
Set up shop
    In the court of law
       Pulled commerce off the street
Tore ideology out the concrete
 Seized the provisions
 Then burnt the money
Cause the money was worthless

42

One night
Prayers, eyes and dreams did meet
The guns
The tanks
The gas
The arms of state
The city is a mercenary
Connected to a cartel
Of citadels
Held together
By murder and mayhem
Chaos and bloodshed
Capital and punishment
Flooded in from every direction
As yet another rebellion was put down by dawn
Then cynically commissioned to paint the city's wall
One night in Camelot
Yet all that is remembered
Is not lost
Long live the hymn of the brick
That escaped the city's wall
The psalm of the flame
That awaits the spark
The Church of the tire iron
Preaching to a choir of Molotovs
Hurled against the law
Myth that is legend
A sense of direction
When you can't trust your senses
Materially
Historic and dialectic
Mysterious until it isn't

It is written for future editions
In the clenched fist of the past
With the timeless message
That there is no time like the present
May take years

May take generations

Then again
May take a night

To Serve Hispanics

Reach for America
Dream for America
Teach
For America
Diversity, equity, inclusion
Access and achievement
USDA certified
STEM
The Department of Defense
The great state of California
Serving as one great big Hispanic Serving Institution
Just imagine
The federal funding
The brochures of underserved
The spreadsheets
Of human misery
The proclamations
Administrations
Boards of trustees
Debating
Safe spaces
For students
To sleep in
Parking lots
Perchance to dream
Of a way of life
That died
Decades before they were born
Debt, debt is the final frontier
And these kids they are America's future

Ronald Reagan's Cold Dead Hands

They close down schools
And build more prisons
They close down schools
And build more prisons
They close down schools
And build more prisons
And then they find ways to fill them
                              Been that way since
                                   Boarding natives
                    Mexicans schools
                         And the white architects
                         Of a Black education
          I am writing this
                                        Mid global pandemic
                    Wherein the rich get rich
                    And the poor get sick
                                        Several generations
in
                                        The twentieth
year
                                        Of the twenty first
century
                                   Twenty twenty shit
Visions of deep shit
          I am writing this
Rapidly approaching
          The eleventh administration
          Of Ronald Reagan
          Wherein the rich get
Offshoring bailouts derivatives
                         Government money to space race
          And the rest get debt
          Homelessness
          And mass incarceration
Then told not to ask why they close down schools build more prisons
                    I only hope this finds you in better times

45

Tumbleweeds

                              And then they said
Something like
                                              You know
More of the world
                    Is covered by tumbleweeds
                                      Than billboards
                  And I said true
But the people live by those signs
                                And I live by the life of the mind
                  And then they said something like
The world is full of life
                        And there is an arrogance to the city
Inherent to industry
                                              The world is burning
And you busy yourself with commercials
                    And I said damn
          The tumbleweeds shall inherit the concrete

Party Hymn

Some say it begins from within
Some say it has already begun
Some say wait upon conditions
Some say inevitable
Some say impossible
Some say it is a process not an event
Some carry signs
Some sign petitions
Some block politicians
Some back politicians
Some become politicians

And I have seen
Academic's metaphysics
Swallow reality
Then spit back a peer reviewed tenure track salary
And I have seen
The organizers of labor
Embrace parties of capital
And I have seen age old cowardice
Dishonesty, careerism
Parade as groundbreakingly new
And I have seen courage
Burst into spontaneous flame
And I have seen fear in the pig's eye
And I have seen rebellions
Light the night sky
Then fade to smoke

Some speak against the need
For political education
Some speak against the need
For party structure and discipline
But I know
Without theory
History does not move
And I know

Once the line is set
Organization is key
That there are decades
For the taking
To be wrenched from weeks
That we cannot wait upon impossible
That none can do it alone
That everyday we must work to make
Victory inevitable
That if we wish to see
Revolution
Within our lifetimes
We must
Organize
Organize
Organize

Everything Between

                    Gas station
               Supermart
                         Food court
          Coffee shop
     Bus stop
          Burrito supreme
               Penny stocks
                         Trust funds
        Check points
  Bailouts
                                             Overdraft fees

Smoke stacks
Minivans
Border fence
Tax shelters
Nuclear debris
        Valley of silicon
               Islands of plastic
                    Burning river pipelines
Food desert landmine
        Jumbo tanks
          Fracking quake
                    The carcinogenic republic of acid rain
          Foggy bottom
                    The world bank
The dying forest
The falling trees
The sky depletes
Over the rising sea
As the horizon greets
Mass extinction

21st Century

Twenty first century

American

Male proletariat

Pushed and prodded

Tried and tested

Pulled in many different directions

Culture

Religion

A boulder

A mountain

The sun in its position

A life lesson

Something his father had taught him

About necktie waterboarding

While force feeding

Coffee and expression

With every man

A king

In a free country

Falling asleep

In front of must-see TV

Hoping

Not to wake to see

Morning in all its wire and concrete

Come rushing from its office

Something

About dreams

Something about

Alarms being set

To something like

You are born

You need

You die

Now surrender

Your life

Sunrise to sunset

Punch in to paycheck

In stolen minutes

              Off the clock

In break rooms

      And barbecues

                 Between celebrations

And cigarettes

          Crisis

        And management

        Terror

             And commitment

Somewhere by the roadside

          Of hollow smiles

              And the deepest

    Saddest, most unrequited of regret

He

   He gets drunk

He gets loud

       Then very, very quiet

Stumbles around

Like

            Questions

               What is my birthright

   To what am I entitled

  And to whom do I owe

What is the value

Of a wasted moment

 And are we truly

  As all

   Alone

    As the night appears to be

Twenty

 First

  Century

  American

   Male

    Proletariat

       Taught something about freedom

Something about ethics

                Independence

            Opportunity

       Citizenship

   A seal

A document
A speech
Or was it a dream

Something

About being judged
By the content of character
Not the color of skin
But that
Was just something
That left him wondering
Why men must be judged at all
And am I truly
My brother's keeper
Or do the rules change in desperation
And if so, why then
Must we abide by them to begin with
And under what pressure
Under what conditions
Is man's character truly formed
And am I really its content
Or merely the documents
Stitched upon birth
To the lining of my pockets
The weight of my wallet
The shirt on my back
And are the stars made of dust

And am I

Made of that
And are those mountains
Not older than nations
And do they weep
With the passing of children
And are we truly alone
With nothing
But the certainty of death
And if so
Why then
Must I spend my life
Shining shoes
Pressing suits
Digging ditches
In preparation
Of my own burial

King of Los Angeles

Head to glass
Fate at hand
Groundless soles
Through the one ways
The one days
The dead ends
And failed beginnings
Of Downtown Los Angeles
When moving at the right speed
It is easy to reimagine
Yourself king
Map out the geography
Claim principality
Over stilted steel
Money stacked so high
Seems like
It belongs
To everyone
It doesn't
Early dawn
Restless feet
Shuffle hand paved streets
As centuries of industry
March into the next
When a man penniless
Says to me
Just my two cents
The fight is fixed
The game is rigged
And the house
Well the house always wins
Which is why you will never find me
Reduced to knees
Bowed
Crouched
Crying out
To the not for profit

Personal lord and savior
Licking the boots
Shining the tombs
Of some long dead founding fathers
Their long dead founding charters
Citing the sacred trust
Of our hallowed institutions
They own the courts
The church
And the constitution
They are steel
We are flesh
They are the law
We are not them
But you
You actually believe
In the things that keep you fed
The world spins
The light of day
Off the cityscape
To my still waking eye
And it's a cruel walk
To the park
But a cool breeze
Off the pond
When gold teeth
Gold rings
Retiree
Says to me
Have a seat
Now here's the first thing
In this game
There are players
And there are pawns
And neither
Escapes the clock
And you
Yes you
You the fool
I could read you
In less the four moves
Open hands

Closed eyes
Open chest
Exposed neck
The charmer
Of hostile snakes
You place your faith
In the hopes of some future embrace
In this world of exchange
Where there are no guarantees
Only hungers to feed
Watch
As they scramble like ducks
At the sight of a few crumbs
Lungs
Have their limits
Power is for the taking
And what is freedom
But the battle cry
Of a man prepared to die
Son I do not believe you
Have it in you
And I remembered
Standing
Before lights flashing
In the shadows
Of mansions
Why lie
I was broke
I was broken
Driver carry me into the night
Poison drives the steel
Money steals the time
Pockets and scars
Fill with the cities exhaust
Of liars
Cynics
Critics
Misers
Drivers
The pride of men
So it is here
In this concrete sea

Of indifference
That I make confession
Sometimes
I imagine
I and I alone
With the power to fix this
Me yes me
The King of Los Angeles
Where none can make it alone
But together
they could not stop us
Night falls
The city breathes
The city speaks
Words simple and complete
Your money
Of your life
Why lie
Why lie
My life
My life
I was born
Free
And penniless
And just like all of you
They have been robbing me
Ever since

Lady Winchester

I.
That is no country for guilty conscience
Laughing, learning in summer near lakes named in remembrance of murder
The young in their way stand as living monuments to generations of forgetting
II.
An aged truth unrenewed is a thing of genocide
The naming of avenue
The making of highway
The forging of boulevard
The foundations of national celebrations, psyches
Bodies of literature
Schools of cinema
Standing in pools of blood
III.
Oh pioneer
This is no place for honest reflection
And I have therefore traveled north
Towards doors and staircases that lead nowhere
Filled with rooms that reach for the dead
Passageways to escape their revenge
IV.
Once I heard the story of Lady Winchester
Building her mansion until the day that she died
In her time a marveled destination
For escape artists
Today sold as mystery to travelers and tourists as curiosity
As to what is past and passing
And they too in their way stand as living monuments
In a home built by rifles
In the great American tradition known
To run from ghosts

Couch Surfing the High Desert

On rare occasion

Heading east to west

On the 210

You may first see them

A few a miles past Azusa

On the 60

Just short of Alhambra

Off the 10

Maybe El Monte

Hanging from the overpass signs

That read NO ICE

In East Los Angeles they are everywhere

By the time you reach the west side

They signs will now read orange man

And not my president

And there is a difference

I want to live in it

I want the eyes

The mind the lens

Of a white liberal

I want to build a life

In that cul-de-sac bubble

In a town you never heard of

Somewhere between

Santa Monica and Malibu

I want to embrace the westside

As it beats its chest

For the clean green way

It moves its trash

To be burned in heaps

In some

Cancer alley southeast

While I keep my

hands clean

As manicured as my neighbor's lawn

And their bleached teeth

White as the Aspen snow

                                        Where I have twice vacationed
                        And I have I seen Paris
                        And I have seen Rome
                        Seen Tokyo, London
        I have even been to the pyramids
                                                        Of Chichen Itza

        But I climbed them as an American
                And there is a difference
                        But this
                                        This not about my time
                        At the top
                                                        Nor is this the epic of
my climb
        Neither is it a tale of woe and collapse
                        Not the tragedy of me losing everything
                                No this the prelude to my comeback foretold
                                                Consider yourself
lucky
For as Seneca said
                                The bravest thing in the world is to see a great man
                Struggle against adversity
                                        And just as you cannot judge a book
                                                                By
its cover
You know nothing of a man
                                Looking only at his setbacks
                                                It is will he commands
That defines his character
        And every day
In one way or another
                                I make my life better
                                        For I am the author of my life
                        Ahead of time
                        I can already tell you the moral of this story
Spoiler alert
                                It is always darkest before the dawn
                                                        This is but prelude
                To the rise of a phoenix
                                                For I am that fire
        I am that rise
                I am that bird
                        Once more I shall fly

                                59

I once had an excellent home
An excellent job
An excellent car
An excellent life
Excellence is a state of mind
And while I might have lost the first two
I know so long as my hands are the wheel
I am headed somewhere better

                              The guest room
             At my recently divorced sister's in Pomona
                                 Is welcoming enough
                 Still I tell her
    This is only temporary
She says her son could use
             The positive influence
       A strong male role model
Though she and I are not
                 Without argument
    First off
After the divorce
       She bought a house less than a driving minute
From our parents
Who does that
She says it is quite common
             She says that I have forgotten
                      Where I come from
       I hold up the driverless fob
   Of my Tesla
And say that is where I am from
And where I plan to return
    Split my time
    Between
   The arts district
  And Claremont Village
              Little known fact about Claremont
          There are more PhDs living there per Capita
          Then anywhere in the United States
              And the Claremonts call themselves
         The Ivy League of the West
          I don't know something to think about
   In the village
There is a record store

For music aficionados

                        And video rental for film connoisseurs

          Records are for teenagers

The cinema is immortal

          Excellence is a state of mind

                    In this time in between careers

I will study the masters

            Of Europe

       Asia

         Africa

            Latin America

          Yes including Mexico

      I have no problem being Mexican

         I just refuse

             To be Mexican in America

Increasingly I find myself

At the library and the café

Routine is important

 And everyday

  In one way or another

            I am making improvements

               Preparing myself for the days ahead

On Sundays

       My sister

         Takes her son to IHOP

     Some nights

         I can be convinced

     To join them

One time

               When she went to the restroom

      I gave the boy some life advice

I tell him

               Each and every one of us is

      Responsible for our outcomes

I tell him

      You are the common denominator of your own world

I tell him

               Each and everyone of us

          Is the author of our own lives

        I then point to the waitress

          And say that will never be me

      Because I work with my mind

When his mother returned

                                        She told me about an opening at her office

                                              The opening pays less than half my old

salary

                    And just a little less than her current

                                        I thank her for her time and concern

I tell her soon I will make my next move

                              Anatoly Karpov once said chess is everything

                  Art, science and sport

            I checked out a book from the library

                And now everyday

              I take my board to the café

                Set up positions

              I studied the night before

          Pretend that I am playing against

       Another master from some distant shore

            Drink several cups of coffee

            Pretending to read several

                                                Papers

                               Journals and periodicals

                            Periodically looking up

                              I eavesdrop

                                For hours

                          On the conversations

                        Of students and professors

                        Getting a free education

                            Before finally

                      Making a single move

                      Then packing up my pieces

           One day when I have mastered this board's secrets

                      I will challenge the learned

                        To a struggle for which they

                            Have not prepared

My sister
Gave me a week to leave her house
Said I was arrogant
Mean and a bad influence
Said she did not want
Her son to grow up
Looking down upon the people
Who served him food
That little shit sold me out

And there is a reason his
Mother never left this town
And there is a reason I did
First chance I got
It's in the zoning
The districts
The redlines
The blueprints
The courthouse
The school system
Off the off ramps
The backs of kitchens
Everyday history everyday
Staring you in the face
But that will never be me
   They say the best lessons in life
   Are the ones learned in defeat
So if I or you or
   Anyone is to learn anything
    From any this
 It's to not neglect your savings
     It's to live within your means
As they say
   Life comes at you fast
     I found space on a couch
    In my price range
   In San Bernardino off craig's list
 I think my roommate
Is some kind of recovering addict

       Health is your number one asset
       Every day I hike Mt. Rubidoux
      Prepare myself for the days ahead
    Some nights I can hear him talking to himself
     Other nights he speaks to me direct
   I try my best to
     Drown out both
        From what I gather
    His wife left with the kids
  From what I gather
     It was with a man he once called his best friend
     A forklift operator somewhere in Fontana
       From what I

gather

They all used to work together so one day
To avoid any awkwardness
To avoid any conflict
To make this transition easy on all of them
He up and quit
Something I would never do
And while I do my best
To avoid conversations
One time this man's crying
Got me so sick to my stomach
I had to say something
I told him
I would have stood my ground
I told him
I would not have given in an inch
I told him
I would never allow
Someone
To come in like that
Snatch up my dreams
Snatch up my life
I told him
That would never be me
That shut him up for about a week
But these thin walls
These thin walls are closing in
Some nights I can hear him
Crying in the shower
Always crying the same thing
He always cries
I always seem to forget
But if I only knew now
What I knew then
I might have been better to them
And now I know I have to leave
I cannot afford to hear any of this
I can already feel
This man's weakness sinking in
Weakness is contagious
And this situation
Is temporary

                    Ever since the Tesla got repossessed
I go for midnight runs
            Everyday
            In one way
            Or another
I am making my life better
                                        Spend most my time in Riverside
                                Near the campus
                Or the Mission Inn
                        Waiting upon the next event
                                            Or Art walk or something
            Where there will be wine and cheese
                                        One day on my hike up Rubidoux
                                As I approached to the mountain top
                I had an epiphany
    It seems
        In all my days I have defined
            My life
                    By my surroundings
                        By the summits I could climb
                        By the worlds I could
                                        Fit myself in
When that light
                    That flight
        That Phoenix
Always burned from within
                                    I am that bird
            As I stare out
                            At the whole Inland Empire
                            I begin think
Man like me

        Place like this
                            I could make the desert bloom

Author's Note: We interrupt this unreliable narration as our protagonist was last seen sixty miles northeast of Hesperia. He has been presumed to have been swallowed by the economy.

Ghost Town

From the Rockies
Through the Owens
Siphoning life
At approximately
Thirteen million
Los Angeles metropolitan
Is a desert metropolis
That ecologically
Probably
Should not exist
Its ports
Monstrous
In dimensions
Vampiric
In practice
This is where the rubber
Meets the first world
As a global proletariat
Of slums and sweatshops
Stock the shelves
Of the American market
Los Angeles
Built on citrus
And munitions
On bracero's sweat
And the making of war
Alpha city
Apex predator
Big bully
But when LA
Tells its tell all
All it can say for itself
Is hurray for Hollywood
Man fuck this place
Times like these
I think of a childhood trip
To Calico

Boom town go bust
Outdoor museum
Silver dust ruins
Ghost town
Times like these
I think of the legend
Of the abandonment
Of Teotihuacan
Some archeologists
Argue drought
Some famine
And the daring argue for rebellion
And I here imagine
A popular uprising
Followed by an exodus
With me leading it
Founding a township of the proletariat
Then as the population expands
States to craft
Powers to enact
The law to enhance
Until the public groans
I've grown
Tyrannical in my rule
And then I am overthrown
By horizontal anarchists
Executed, beheaded
With final words
Democratic centralism
Escaping my scientific
Ruby red lips
Now victorious
The horizontalists
Promise and deliver
Upon a summer of love
And an autumn of chill
Which quickly gives way
To a winter of discontent
As the anarchists split
Disconnect into affinity groups
Later co ops
And finally divide

Into bureaucrats and venture capitalists
Until the day the newly minted rich
Find themselves at the short end of the guillotine
A footnote
Under the mighty boot
Of the Sedillista army
Once the dictatorship of the proletariat
Is reestablished
A statue of my likeness and in my honor will be erected
At the center of all things
Only to be torn down again in roughly three generations
As the whole process begins again
At least that's how I imagine it

Cheney's Sparrows

Let's take a trip
Around the globe
Tripoli for the coast
Guam for the beaches
Puerto Rico for the sands
Cuba for the sugar
El Salvador for the coffee
Chile for the copper
Mexico for the land
Haiti for the debt
Indonesia for the sweat
The Soviet Union for
The bad example that might set
The Congo for the coltan
Angola for the diamonds
Bolivia for the lithium
Samoa for the base
Panama for the canal
Colombia for the cane
Yugoslavia
I mean Serbia
I mean Kosovo
For the zinc
The Philippines
Just bout everything
Nicaragua
Guatemala
Costa Rica
Honduras
the Dominican Republic
Its bananas
China for the opium
Or at least a piece of the trade
Afghanistan for the poppies
The more things change
Somalia
Venezuela

Libya
Yemen
Iraq
Iran
The shiny new
South Sudan
C'mon kids
You know what is
Eighty nations
Eight hundred bases
It's that mighty mighty
United States
Greatest Democracy on earth
On a tour de force
We're talking rifles
Helmets
No bid contracts
Cavalier vests
Stealth jets
Carriers
Cost plus percentage
War is not a racket
It's the wealth of nations
It's the spoils of victory
The measure of centuries
Historical memory
And when you are long forgotten
All used up
Traumatized by the unspeakable things
You have done
Enriching people you will never meet
Dick Cheney
Will outlive us all
Still sending Christmas cards
To his rich and powerful friends
Waxing poetic
About sparrows and empires
And when that happens
And when it hurts
And it will hurt
I want you to remember
That men like Dick Cheney

Could not have accomplished a single thing
Without little expendable toy soldiers
Just like yourself
And isn't that something
Isn't that to write home about

If 2020 was an election

In case you haven't noticed
The air is toxic
  The water is poison
    The elections are racket
                An empty bucket
  Hurled towards
          A burning house
          We call politics
          With billions on the line

                                    Behind closed doors
                              Lobbyists
                                              Politicians
                                Disembodied corporations
                  Make the decisions
        That cage millions
                  Then stage a debate
                            On the house floor
                      As though their settled vote
                      Had not been cast
                      Centuries before
                      This is some Plymouth shit
                                    Some Dixieland
                            Some Wild Wild West
                            America twists again
                            Like it did last cold war
                            American intelligence
Will preemptively blame
                      Chinese or Russian
Interference for the results
                              Of an election
                                    Wherein half the population
Will not vote
                        Decided by an electoral college
                              Meaning the actual count of votes
Will not count
                        The American media
    Will blame unarmed Black men

72

                        For being shot by police unions
                                Police unions will blame anyone
with a cell phone
            For recording the incident
                                American governors will blame Brown workers
            For a global pandemic
                        And the American public will blame the rest of the globe
            For being bombed by America
If 2020 were an election
It would star Joe Biden
Challenging incumbent Donald Trump
Some red states
Some blue states
The US senate
New York real estate
Kids in cages
Knees on the necks
A border wall
A border fence
A bipartisan shot in the legs
A segregationist
A dixiecrat
A dance with two devils
As the country burns to the ground
In case you hadn't fucking noticed

The Straw

1 INT: JOVEN CISNEROS ALONE IN HOTEL
The bed is neatly made and Joven's suits are finely pressed, we hear the faucet
in another room. We then hear the faucet running, closing in on the sink. His
toothbrush and hand enter shot as toothbrush is watered. We stay on the sink as
the water continues to run. We hear the sounds of him brushing his teeth. We
get our first shot of Joven. We see him spit into the faucet then his hands cupping
water to splash his face. He dries his face and stares into mirror. He speaks.
Joven Cisneros
I am Joven Cisneros, next duly elected President of the Republic of the Middle Class.
 (SCREEN FADES TO BLACK AND WHITE LETTERING COMES IN
FROM BOTTOM TO TOP)
The year is 2240 two hundred years after the great renaming wherein the
United States of America bowing to political pressure of demographic demands
changed its name to the Republic of the Middle Class. In the aftermath both
the Republican and Democratic parties were dissolved as elements and figures
from both parties splintered off into many political formations. After two
elections again two major parties emerged. The Jobs Party and the Party of Jesus
Plus Nothing. The heated debates between these two groups led to the Last
American War. Leading up to the Great Renaming then President Jeff Bezos
waged a space race against then Governor of Semi-Autonomous California
Elon Musk to colonize Mars. Musk had landed first but had made many gross
miscalculations and his colony was saved from disaster by Bezos who then
claimed and expanded the colony. During the last American war nearly half of
America's billionaires fled the planet for the moon. After the war the Jobs party
emerged victorious. The party's first major action taken was the Job Creators
Accord, a stipulation that made it illegal to become a billionaire. Following the
accord, once individuals' net worth would reach a billion dollars their assets
on Earth liquidated and they would be compensated but forced to live on the
moon colony as a Job Creator. For nearly one hundred years the Jobs Party had
a single party sway over the Republic of the Middle Class until the convention
of 2136 at which time the party split in two eventually becoming the Traditional
Jobs Party and the Party of Innovation. In 2240 The Party of Innovation was in
power for 12 years. The signature project of this time for the party has been a
jobs program around the construction of a straw to drain the great lakes in order

to service the moon. This project began under an administration of Traditional Jobs Party under the now disgraced Mike Kim presidency. The project has stalled for reasons of bipartisan graft and corruption but also because of the scientific challenges of such an undertaking. The Traditional Jobs party sees opportunity to regain power given the failure of The Party of Innovation to deliver on construction of the straw. There is no debate as to whether the straw should be built.

2 INT. GINGER AND JOVEN IN ROOM

Ginger Roman

Oh don't watch that c'mon you are torturing yourself…..

3 INT. TELEVISION

Shot of screen with straw protestors sign reads "This is the final straw" other signs present but blurry

Joven Cisneros

Someone must be funding them.

Ginger Roman

Local yokels everywhere across the country. God damn confederation of peanut galleries. It's that damn Bernardo Sanchez. It's that goddamn Bernardo Sanchez wave. Sanchez is the one riling them up that crazy old disheveled fuck.

Joven Cisneros

Bernardo Sanchez is in favor of the straw.

Ginger Roman

{gestures to television}

Fuck your straw?! I mean how is that even a joke you seahorse losers. Where's the set up? Where's the punchline? What am I looking at here?

Joven Cisneros

It's a protest sign

Ginger Roman

Where's the hint of irony? What are they trying to imply anyway?

Joven Cisneros

Enough.

Ginger Roman

We got to tie these dirty water fucks to the Sanchez campaign

Joven Cisneros

The Sanchez campaign wants to build the straw. Bernardo Sanchez backs the straw.

Ginger Roman

With reservations and misgivings.

Joven Cisneros

This Republic was rebuilt on reservations and misgivings. This party was built on reservations and misgivings. This party embodies the values of the Republic far more than any other party has ever existed in our short but proud history. And I embody the values of this party far more than the other candidates. That is why I will win. That is why I should lead.

Ginger Roman

Yeah but good old Bernardo wrote his misgivings down.

Joven Cisneros

And another thing, I too have misgivings and reservations about the straw. I have misgivings and reservations about virtually everything.

Ginger Roman

Sanchez wrote his official reservations and misgivings down in detail. Point by point and released them to the public. That's the difference.

Joven Cisneros

That was excessive. I grant you that that was excessive.

Ginger Roman

Dangerous even

Joven Cisneros

Now you are being excessive. Bernardo Sanchez has also gone on record and wants to build the straw. He just wants it built the right way. With correct government oversight and provisions and coordination with the job creators. That is the official party position and though he skirts the line he is still well within party loyalty for the most part.

Ginger Roman

You think anyone reads his shit? I know I didn't. Did you?

Joven Cisneros

I intend to after the election. I don't know if you have noticed but I am a bit tied up at the moment.

Ginger Roman

Then you have no idea how excessive or moderate he is. And you are not alone in that. No one does. No one reads what he writes. The Middle Class doesn't read. No one cares about his speeches beyond a soundbite. It's what he represents. And what he represents is what we are sorely lacking, Mr. Pressed. Substance.

(shot of the TV protestor holding sign "Cisneros is a Straw Man")

        Ginger Roman continue

But it's a gooey substance. A gooey substance of lying. He goes around lying to the Middle Class. Making promises. Just promising things. Making promises.

He's making promises. Making promises. Promising things that the job creators would ever approve of. No they would not. And then what do you have? A god damn government out of sink with commerce. So that would never happen. Will never happen. But he is allowed to compete with us. The Trads would deal with him no fuss no muss. But we have to suffer this insufferable king of the unscrubbed. And how do you compete with that? You can't compete with that. You can't compete with a willing and wanton liar. You can't compete with a man who loves to lie for applause. Bernardo Sanchez is to lies what trained seals are to tricks. Who knows what he will say next!

Joven Cisneros

Bernardo Sanchez is not a trained seal.

Ginger Roman

Clearly not

Joven Cisneros

And while we have our differences.

Ginger Roman

Could use some training. This rebellious otter.

Joven Cisneros

And while we have our differences, while we have our differences, Sanchez is an important part of this party. He is rounding up the disaffected. They listen to him. He is pulling in the wayward, misled those given to excesses. He is letting them know there is a place for them here in our big tent. From there the rest of us can pull them to the truth of our party, the middle of the road for the middle class. That is our job. Not his. He is doing his job. We must do ours.

Ginger Roman

Bernardo Sanchez is a feral con man who wrote his reservations down in detail and made them public.

Joven Cisneros

Yes, that is excessive.

Ginger Roman

Dangerous. And that's the difference. That's the problem. You have an authenticity gap, an enthusiasm gap and a danger gap.

Joven Cisneros

Solution?

Ginger Roman

I don't know yet

Joven Cisneros

Don't mention it again until you do. Problem?

Ginger Roman

The Bernadettes think the primary is rigged against Sanchez.

Joven Cisneros

The purpose of the Supreme College must be better explained to the Middle Class

Ginger Roman

Those kinds of explanations will have to wait until after the election. If we make that a talking point now and you can just forget about…

Joven Cisneros

No need to finish your sentence. I already agree.

Ginger Roman

Alright. I knew you had some strategy in you. You asked about those hydro terrorists. What if we can pin a foreign hand to Bernardo and his decision-making process? A few whispers to our friends in the newsrooms.

Joven Cisneros

I am only going to say this once. And I will not say this again. You will not do that.

Ginger Roman

Sanchez is out there riling up terrorist bums lying to the Middle Class and you are worried about his good name.

Joven Cisneros

I am beating him aren't I?

Ginger Roman

You don't really want to solve this problem. You are going to win. If all else fails the Supreme College will see to that. The Guardians of Democracy are already suppressing his algorithms. We can count on Rodriguez-Rodriguez Cheng for that. But when it comes to the general. I am not sure the Guardians will be on our side. So we will win the primary. But it's how you win the primary that will determine your chances in the general. You beat everyone else but with Sanchez you are already getting more than a little help from the Supreme College. We need to trounce this guy. Smash him into dirt and have him praise your name.

Joven Cisneros

Everyone agrees he is excessive.

Ginger Roman

Everyone but his supporters. Listen Mr. Pressed. You are charismatic. But you are charismatic because you are handsome. You seem decent. But you seem decent because you actually believe in all this shit. I mean a fucking straw to the moon. I mean think about it, I mean really think about it. That shit is crazy. Will it even work? What the fuck are we doing? Why the fuck are we doing this? But you, you never stop to ask questions like that. You never stop to ask anything! You just ask how, where and when. You don't ask why. You don't ask what. Fuck that! You just push forward. You carry out the program. That's the you I know. And that's the you the middle class needs to be reminded of. That's why you should lead and that's what the middle class needs to see. A leader. A steady hand in uncertain times. In uncertain times or even certain doom the hand of Joven Cisneros does not waver! That is what they want to see, that is what they need to hear!

Joven Cisneros

I believe in the straw

Ginger Roman

I know you do. But this isn't about the straw, this is about Sanchez and his band of hydro squatters. And right now we are dealing with major gaps. We are dealing with an authenticity gap, an enthusiasm gap, a danger gap. And if you think this is bad. I am telling you now. The newsrooms have it all wrong. Gail Kim is going to win her primary. And she represents a level of badass you have never been up against Mr. Pressed.

Joven Cisneros

Do you really think she will win?

Ginger Roman

You watch by the time she comes through, no talking point about the failure of the Trads will work. It will all be about the Kim dynasty. Her, her father, the Straw legacy. And Bernardo, after he has been beaten, Sanchez won't go away. I mean he will say he backs you, just like he backs every frontrunner after losing. But he will never stop and neither will his liquid cult. We will be facing the Trads from the right and Sanchezismo from the left. And when that happens, I can't have you talking that old middling shit. There is a demon in your eyes, just waiting to get out! I need you to unleash that beast! Let that tiger out of his cage. Stop talking sweet.

Joven Cisneros

Are you done?

Ginger Roman

Am I done? I am just getting started, where was I? Talking sweet. Coming across like a honey bear talking that old shit. The year is 2240, no one is ordering that lukewarm porridge. Goldilocks is dead! And those fucking bears ate her alive!

INT 4 TELEVISION

Protestor sign reads "The Straw that Broke the Republic's Back"

END SCENE

BEGIN SCENE
INT 1 JOVEN CISNEROS GINGER ROMAN AND JENNIFER CHEN

ALL ON BUS PREPARING FOR OPENING REMARKS AT DEBATE
WITH GAIL KIM)

Joven Cisneros
The middle class deserves answers
Ginger Roman
Boring!!!
Jennifer Chen
I don't see how yelling boring is helpful
Ginger Roman
I don't see how writing boring speeches is helpful
Joven Cisneros
Will you stop?
Ginger Roman
I'll stop when you stop. Stop boring me. Look, listen I am begging you here.
I am pleading. On bended knee on my last legs with a torn rotator, a bruised
rib, a chipped nail and a broken heart. I am begging you. Listen, please. Please.
Please, please work with me. I am begging you here. Please work with me.
Jennifer Chen
Are we still drug testing?
Ginger Roman
These talking points. They are shit. They are cliché and worse yet they are
shit. And worse yet they are stiff. Stiff shit. And worst of all, boring. And
boring won't cut it. Not this year. Not with history calling. We have a historical
opportunity. You hear that? You hear that? History is sounding the alarm and
you are hitting the snooze. You hear that? You hear that? That is the sound of
Gail Kim answering the phone. Booking a work lunch with history. You think
this is bad? You think this abuse?
Jennifer Chen
I think it is pointless
Ginger Roman
Have you seen your opponent? Have you seen Gail Kim? The Middle Class loves
her. The Middle Class does not want to hear the old talking points. They want
to hear fresh new takes on the same old bullshit. Find another way of saying the
same shit.
Joven Cisneros
And you want to write my speeches? With that attitude?
Ginger Roman
No. That is not what I was hired to do. That is Jennifer's job.

80

Jennifer Chen
You waste a lot of time with this bullshit.
Ginger Roman
I think I might have to though. I think I just might have to. I think I might have to write the speeches. I mean listen to yourself, the Middle Class deserves better, the Middle Class deserves answers. The Middle Class knows damn well they don't have a damn thing coming and that is damned sight better than they damn well they deserve. And they fucking know it. And the least you can do is not bore them. Do your job. They do theirs. Give them a good floor show. The speech is the job.
Jennifer Chen
A cynic. You're a cynic. How is cynicism helpful?
Joven Cisneros
Cynicism is the most cancerous of all excesses.
Ginger Roman
Call it what you want. I earned my spot on this bus by winning.
Jennifer Chen
I don't care what you have done in the past. Right now you are practicing cynicism.
Ginger Roman
In all my years of public service no one has once called me a cynic.
Joven Cisneros
No one is calling you a cynic.
Jennifer Chen
I did not call you a cynic, I said you are slipping into cynicism.
Ginger Roman
If that is how you feel about me Joven I will resign right now.
Joven Cisneros
No one is called you a cynic, just that your statements could be construed as cynical.
Ginger Roman
I have served this party my entire adult life with loyalty. I grew up at this party. And never once has someone called me that word.
Jennifer Chen
No one called you a cynic!!! Just that what you were saying might be misconstrued as a cynical posture!
Ginger Roman
You called me a cynic!!! Don't lie about it now!!!
Jennifer Chen
Don't put words in my mouth I said what you were saying could be interpreted as cynicism

Ginger Roman

I know I have my excesses but I am no cynic!!! Nor I am a liar which is more than I can say for you!!!

Jennifer Chen

So I am a liar now?

Joven Cisneros

(Camera changes to point of view of Joven world begins to blur both Jennifer and Ginger are talking though we can't clearly make out either Joven's inner dialogue speaks saying "I am going to say this is banter")

Jennifer Chen (continue)

.... I am sorry you feel that way but I said you were being cynical not that you are a cynic

Joven Cisneros

Banter. This is banter. Banter is good. Banter is fine. Banter is creative. Banter gets the creative juices flowing. But like all things banter must be done in moderation. Let's just say any perceived insult was merely banter.

Jennifer Chen

I can punch it up. We can punch it up. The speech can be worked out. That's all you had to say Ginger. The speech needs work. We are racing against the clock. These antics of yours aren't helping anything. Point taken, we can punch up the speech.

Joven Cisneros

Seems one of you is ready to work. How about the other?

Jennifer Chen

Could save a lot of time this way you know. Much less stress. You know, helpful.

Ginger Roman

Fine, I am ready to work. Alright then go on. (awkward silence) With the speech go on with opening remarks.

Jennifer Chen

No forget it

Ginger Roman

No go on

Joven Cisneros

And the Party of Innovation has those answers

Ginger Roman

Oh sweet fucking drill to the temple!!!

Jennifer Chen

Alright you know what? Forget the speech. Just forget it. I'll draft up something new. Something from scratch

Joven Cisneros
We all only have two weeks
Ginger Roman
Yeah that's a problem
Joven Cisneros
It is a problem
Ginger Roman
The problem is
Joven Cisneros
Jennifer. I want to hear from Jennifer. You have spoken enough already
Ginger Roman
That is my job.
Joven Cisneros
Your job is to win. For the time being that is all of our jobs. Jennifer. Problem?
Jennifer Chen
Gail Kim is formidable. In many people's minds the Traditional Jobs Party
corruption scandals are no longer the issue. The failure to build the straw is
now on us, on red tape, bureaucracy, both parties and frankly anyone not
named Kim. She has pivoted heavily into the legacy of her father as someone
who got things done. She's playing up the corruption scandals of her father's
administration as the conspiracies of what she calls "the jealous and poorly
dressed" as well as "pencil pushing little men."
Ginger Roman
Oh that's wonderful
Jennifer Chen
Why are you on this bus?
Ginger Roman
To win
Joven Cisneros
Don't interrupt. Continue.
Jennifer Chen
Everything that would normally disqualify a candidate she plays into as a
strength.
Ginger Roman
And how is that working out for her?
Jennifer Chen
She won her primary.
Ginger Roman
Keep going in this direction and she is going to win the general too.

Joven Cisneros
Solution? (long silence)
Jennifer Chen
That is kind of a big question. That is kind of the whole campaign.
Ginger Roman
She doesn't know and neither do you Mr. Pressed. I know what it takes and neither of you are willing to listen much less do it.
Jennifer Chen
I am so glad that I made the decision early on that I was not going to pretend to like you.
Ginger Roman
Well that's a shame. Cause I like you just fine. Your speeches could use some work. Hurts me to say. Really tears me up inside.
Jennifer Chen
All I am saying is it would be really awkward for us both if I had to hide just how deeply I truly hate you.
Ginger Roman
Is this the part where you call me a cynic again?
Jennifer Chen
I never called you a cynic. I said you were being cynical
Ginger Roman
You know I may have some excesses but lying...
Jennifer Chen
Oh so I am a liar.
(camera returns to Joven's point of you vision begins to blur can see images can see Jennifer and Ginger arguing animated) (Joven's internal monologue "I am going to headbutt him")
Joven Cisneros
That's enough out of you!!! (grabs Ginger by lapels ginger wrestles a bit left to right)
Ginger Roman
NO MR. PRESSED!!! NO!!!
Joven Cisneros
(Slaps Ginger and after their heads align headbutts him before throwing him to the ground) (Joven regains composure after a few deep breaths)
I feel better already. (pauses) Jennifer I am sorry you had to see that.
Jennifer Chen
No. I loved it. Found it quite refreshing actually.
Ginger Roman
You see what I mean??!! She loved it!!! And so will the Middle Class!!! You are

animal Cisneros!!! Not a straw man for straw times but a beast of the wild!!! You are barely contained bucket of rage Mr. Pressed!!! there is something inside of you!!! Something scary!!! Something burning!!! Burning at industrial strength!!! Mr. Pressed!!! You are not weak like the rest of us!!! Looking for direction!!! Crying in the dark!!! Hobbling through the night!!! When you set your mind to do something you do it!!! You want to run a race!!! You win a race!!! You want to head butt a man, that man is going to the ground!!! And if you want to build a straw I pity anything that breathes that stands in your way!!! You got machine gun oil for blood Mr. Pressed!!! You got crude oil running through your veins!!! Oozing out your pores!!! Beaming out your sockets!!! And that's what we need to bring to the opening comments Mr. Pressed!!! Get that oil out there!!! You are gonna be firing that crude oil off in every direction!!! In the front row and in the back row and of course right down the middle!!! Miss a spot??!! Miss a spot!!? Who are they playing with?!! Who are they talking about??!! Joven Cisneros doesn't miss a spot!!! Joven Cisneros let people slip sliding down the aisles!!! We are gonna have to bottle that crude oil!!! Package it, label it, bottle it and give it to the Middle Class!!! And once we do we will go up to those hydro bums and say drink it up you eco barbarians and they will say (in a mocking voice) "no that's crude oil you can't make us drink that" and we will say "get a job you water scum!!! Drink it up!!!" and then we are gonna make straws with your fucking name on it!!! Campaign straws that say Joven Cisneros!!! Get them out there with the bottles so the middle class knows Joven Cisneros knows how to build a fucking straw!!!

END SCENE

BEGIN SCENE

INT 1 JOVEN CISNEROS, JENNIFER CHEN AND GINGER ROMAN AT CAMPAIGN RALLY HOURS BEFORE IT BEGINS TWO DAYS AWAY FROM DEBATE

Joven Cisneros
Are you ready?
Jennifer Chen
You'll like this, we channeled you.
Ginger Roman
There's only one Ginger Roman
Jennifer Chen
Thankfully

85

Ginger Roman

Alright enough bullshit

Jennifer Chen

Oh mr. professional

Ginger Roman

C'mon

Joven Cisneros

Alright, alright, (clears throat)

Thank you, fill in the blank, it is an honor to be here at the university of the middle class in historic Michigan so near to the commissioning of the straw. Blah blah fill in the blank fill in the blank.... alright here we go....

The Great Renaming. The Last American war. The Job Creator Accords. The Party Split. Night of the Cynics. The establishment of the Guardians of Democracy. And of course the Commissioning Of The Straw. All defining moments of our young republic. And believe it or not here we find ourselves once more at the crossroads of history. The decisions we make in the upcoming election will not only define the lives of individuals. This decision will define the life of a nation.

We are at a fork in the road. One road is the road of cynicism, paved with overly philosophical inquiry, loaded intentions and the asking of questions that have no answers. The cynics say there is no choice. That we are all empty suits. That one politician is no different than the next. Straw men for straw polls for a straw era. The cynic says our choices do not matter. This is the height of cynicism. Our choice is our voice. And our voices matter.

On the other hand, there is the road excess littered by reckless abandon. It is a road that misleads towards unintended consequence and unforeseen ruin. This is the path Gail Kim threatens to lead us down.

But I propose a third way. A third road. A middle road. The middle road for the middle class. That proud and still functioning path paved with the wisdom that this republic was founded on. Moderation. Moderation. Moderation.

I have not come here to lead you. Nor have I come to wait upon polls just to trail behind. I am here as a proud member of the middle class prepared to roll up my sleeves and walk beside you. For there is nothing to be so cynical about but cynicism itself. And I implore you to ask not what can the republic do for the middle class, ask what can the middle class do for the republic. For there is nothing so wrong with the republic that cannot be fixed with what is right about the middle class.

We are the middle class. We are the middle class and we will never be immobilized by doubt, or malaise or too much analysis. We do not sit around waiting for rain. We do not scratch our heads either. We roll up our sleeves. We know what we are doing and we know why we are doing it. We don't ask what or why. We ask how and when. We are not cynics. We don't ask why we are doing this? We don't ask will it work? We don't ask why do the job creators live on the moon? Where else would they live? On a melting glacier?! We are the middle class and it is only after the when and the how have been answered that we even begin to entertain the question of why and what. And when we do ask what, we ask only what is next for our Republic.

Our republic, our grand republic. What do all our defining moments have in common? The good and common sense of the middle class. The wisdom of knowing when it is time for a course correction and the wisdom to know when it is time to stay the course.

The 20th and 21st century were times of horrific excess. A time of nuclear barbarism. A time of Bolsheviks and billionaires. A time when men like Fidel Castro and Donald Trump roamed the earth. But those political ideologies and the movements they represented have long gone the way of the dinosaur. Struck down by the meteor of middle class moderation.

Gail Kim threatens a return to those excesses. She says not only in her first year will she complete the building of the straw but also by the end of her first term, drain the build a series of straws capable of draining all our fresh water reserves dry. Since the moment she campaigned on this promise countless scientific articles in countless scientific journals, some signed off on by the job creators themselves, have said why that might not be such a good idea. But you don't need to read scientific journals to know that. You are the middle class. You know excess when you see it, a bad idea when you hear one and can build the greatest straw known to man should you have a hand in shaping it. Gail Kim says she will build a series of straws powerful enough to swallow the ocean in a single gulp. I say, at least until we know more, just a sip. Gail Kim says she will build this straw within one year. I say we will build a straw that will last a millennium. Doing it our way. The right way. The middle road for the Middle Class. Moderation. Moderation. Moderation.

That's it

Ginger Roman
You wrote that?
Jennifer Chen
Me and the boss, mostly me, me being you
Ginger Roman

That's incredible Jennifer. I am sorry I ever doubted you.
Jennifer Chen
I am sorry I called you a cynic.
Ginger Roman
You fucking did
Jennifer Chen
I know I did
Ginger Roman
The speech is amazing. And your delivery
Joven Cisneros
And it has the added bonus that I believe every word of it
Ginger Roman
Well Mr. Pressed. Or should I say Mr. President. You have made a believer out of me.

END SCENE

Last Night I Dreamt I was Vladimir Lenin

Last night I dreamt I was Vladimir Lenin
Grainy and cross cut

In a three-piece classic
Like something out of Potemkin
One minute before a cheering audience
And then in the next
In clever disguise
Crossing rail lines
Smuggling ideas
Shaking the world
In Invisible ink
Across nations
Borders
Bourgeoisies
Denouncing
Social democrats
Caviar still fresh on their breath
Last night I dreamt
I wrestled a revolution
Out of the hands of such men
United all the proletariat
Of all the Russias
And at every step
I knew exactly
What was to be done
I woke in cold sweat
Who was I
Who lived life in such uncertain way
To dream of such things
Confused and ashamed
I turned my head
Drifted back to sleep
Last I dreamt I was Mao Zedong
And it was a two line struggle
Against imperialists
And interparty politics
Convincing landlords

To lay down their arms
Join the long march
Or lay down their life
Succeeding where
Boxer rebellions
Ninety eleven
And the first attempts
At the Chinese republic
Fell
And everywhere there was combat
Last night
I dreamt of
Pain and deprivation
Hunger and humiliation
Centuries
Of dynasties
Addictions
Sacrifice
And service
Principle
And courage
Example
And leadership
Awakened strength
Fearless and forward I dreamt
We leapt
And again I woke in a cold sweat
Confused and ashamed
Who was I
Who lived life
In such a selfish way
To dream of such things
A community college dropout
Who had seen the wrong side
Of eviction notices
DUI Convictions
Couchsurfing
Homeless
Who was I
Who couldn't even
Manage first and last month's rent
Who chased all life's sorrows and misery

To the bottle's end
To dream of leading nations
Last night I dreamt
I was Fidel Castro
In solitary confinement
Having failed
To take Moncada
Awaiting
What would come next
Life imprisonment
Death sentence
Secret execution
Wherein
I would never be heard from again
Perhaps
Destined for unmarked grave
Brought in on criminal charges
By a criminal state
It was then
I held dearest
To my convictions
My commitments
Last night I dreamt
I was Fidel
And I was scared
I did not want to die
Having the enemy
Bury me in a shroud of lies
The truth
There is a truth
A truth that burns brighter than fascism
It is a light
That cannot be extinguished
By bayonets
History would absolve me
Because you can kill a man
But not an idea
Whose time has come
Last night I dreamt
I was el comandante
Returning to Cuba
After years of exile

With only twenty surviving men
Gathered in the Sierra Maestra
Three words on my breath
Batista is fucked
Last night I dreamt
After countless failures
Tragic missteps
Unforeseen setbacks
Armed principally
With courage
And conviction
I successfully led
The Cuban Revolution
And I woke
Seven years sober
Knowing the worlds of difference
Between dreams and a plan
But that nothing began
Without a vision
Without some small conceit
That even the mighty oak
Grew from the smallest of seeds
That a Vietnamese cook
Living in Paris at the time
Stormed the treaty of Versailles
Demanding independence for his nation
That a farmer
Rancher
Horseman
Fighting local disputes
Would teach the whole world
That is better to die on your feet
Than live on your knees
That whatever the meaning
Of these passing dreams
I seek to live my life as that seed
As a pair of feet
As a voice in the choir
A hand on the banner
Raised proudly
Raised defiantly
Raised to the very last of me

May your enemies
Live in interesting times
May a bright shining path
Illuminate your life
May you speak
With courage and conviction
May you dream
Of extraordinary things
And may your every breath
Forward the revolution

The Sea

Whatever it is we are doing
It is only making the storm stronger
There is land under the water
And there too we drill
Capitalists dream of bottomless pits
Then piss and shit the bed plastic
All life began in the ocean
And there too we kill
There are mountains under the water
Cities too I imagine
Arrogant and delusional
One day the sea will swallow us whole

BONUS MATERIALS

The U$

The U$ has

Not enough beds

                Too many yachts

Not enough masks

                Too many tanks

Not enough masks
No supply
All demand

        The U$ has

                Too many loopholes

Not enough homes

                Too many billionaires

Not enough ventilators

                Too much private sector

No
Public infrastructure
To speak of

                Too many tax cuts

Not enough gloves
Far too much cover up

                The richest nation on earth

        Just as it was designed

To be

         Unending
         Unbending
         Production line

                Of war
                Famine
                Disease

Anthem

On the day the world burned to the ground
America flew the flag at half-mast
Limited edition
Embossed proud bald eagles
In the form
Of memorabilia coins
Were sold
To the sounds of taps on a bugle
As stadiums filled with hearts at hand
Willing to die for what they believed
All pledging allegiance to the bitter end
All proud brave Americans willing to die for free

Capital is a Death Cult

Every time
A capitalist dies
Life insured
By banking trust
An inheritance is born
Capital is dead labor
Born buried alive
In the dirt of yesteryear
Personified calculations
Dawn the mask of worker
Pour sweat
Into assembly
Until all existence is doubled
And all purpose is split
Across grids
And spreadsheets of expense
As Proletarian limbs
Move like digits
Ducking and dodging
Bobbing and weaving
The downside of downsize
And the quicksand of debt
In their free time
They attempt to stretch
Some
Meaning
Out of something
That is theirs alone
Their best is generally kept
For grandkids
At the knee
Or for funeral speech
Some pray for a steady hand
Some for a second chance
Others simply for a quick end
And there are dreams
Everywhere

And every mind is a universe
And in the blink of an eye
Any one of them
Could be someone
Somewhere else
This is the secret life of statistics
As they are eaten alive
By accounting machines
The capital crime goes unpunished
Hardly noticed
They just keep moving
To a morbid chant of survival
In an ugly dance of conviction
As they discipline
Any sign of dissent
That might arise from within them
Instead of rising up
They praise the rich
In the midst
Of a global pandemic
They praise illusions
So obvious
They are should be embarrassment
To all who hear and speak them
How will future generations see us
What does it matter
The dead know no shame
Capital is a death cult

About the Author

Matt Sedillo has been described as the "best political poet in America" as well as "the poet laureate of the struggle" by academics, poets, and journalists alike. He has appeared on CSPAN and has been featured in the *Los Angeles Times*, among other publications. He has spoken at Casa de las Americas in Havana, Cuba, at numerous conferences and forums such as the National Conference on Race & Ethnicity in American Higher Education, and at over a hundred universities and colleges, including the University of Cambridge and many others. He is the current literary director of the dA Center for the Arts and author of *Mowing Leaves of Grass* (Flowersong Press, 2019), which is currently being taught at California State University at Northridge and Monterey Bay, as well as at Mission College. His Three Act Poem structure has been taught as capstones of coursework at UCLA and Occidental College. His collection *Mowing Leaves of Grass* (FlowerSong Press 2019) is being taught in classrooms nationwide.